Living on the Edge

poems by

Deborah C. Linker

SeaStory Press
Key West, Florida

Living on the Edge
© 2012 by Deborah C. Linker
All rights reserved
Reproduction of this book or any part thereof is prohibited, except for quotation for review purposes, without express permission of the author and publisher.
Printed in the United States of America
ISBN 978-1-936818-31-0
LCCN 20122937310

Cover photography by Liz Montgomery

SeaStory Press
305 Whitehead St. #1
Key West. Florida 33040
www.seastorypress.com

For my father, who shared
his love of water, and introduced me
to this wonderful paradise – the Florida Keys

Robert W. Crutcher
April 28, 1918 – September 24, 2007

Acknowledgements

My sincere gratitude to my dear friend, Leonel Valle, who without his inspiration, encouragement, and talent this book would never have been published.

A big thanks to the Nancys in my life, Nancy Desmond and Nancy Spence for their eagle eyes and support while I re-invented myself and of course thanks to my irreplaceable friend of over fifty years, Teresa, who believes in me no matter what I attempt.

Finally, I wish to thank my fellow authors of the "Big Pine Writer's Group" who gave me honest, helpful critiques, and pushed me forward.

Introduction

I first traveled to the Florida Keys in the 1960s, when my family spent Christmas vacations fishing, water skiing, soaking up the warm sunshine and reveling in the tropical breezes of Marathon. Each year I returned home to Western Kentucky boasting a mid-winter tan and dreaming of one day living in this paradise. Now, I am lucky enough to call the Florida Keys my home.

This collection of poems is a reflection of my journey through loss, love, and recovery with the theme of beauty and nature of my surroundings. I came to the Keys because of the water, I stayed for the people. Not only am I attracted to the welcoming community I live in today, but I am inspired by the strong-willed, independent pioneers who struggled to survive in the harsh environment of the Florida Keys. I believe their spirit is the foundation of the characters of today —

>   Living on the edge
>   of the world
>   the sea
>   of life
>   on razor's edge
>   of emotion
>   love
>   loss
>   the edge —

Contents

Acknowledgements	vii
Introduction	ix
Contents	x
Living On the Edge	1
Orchids at Midnight	2
Listen	3
Fear	4
Coming Home	6
Strong as Lily	8
Bonsai	10
Slack Tide	11
Sounds Without Borders	12
Romance	13
Mighty Osprey	14
Gonna Fly	15
The Boss	16
Sunset Dreams	17
Nickerbean	18
China	19
Vanishing	20
Quiet Love	21
As You Sleep	22
Still Stalking	23
Last Time I Cried	24
Salty Queen	26

Contents

Nourishment	28
Seasoned Passion	29
Mentor	32
Before Dawn	34
For Charlie	35
Carrousel of Life	36
Shattered	38
Last Hug	39
Cold Bed	40
Deadly Manchineel	41
Late Night Lover	42
Turning Fifty-Nine	44
Chillin' in the Keys	45
About the Author	46
Resources	47

"Poetry is a life-cherishing force. For poems are not words, after all, but fires for the cold, ropes let down to the lost, something as necessary as bread in the pockets of the hungry. Yes, indeed."

—*A Poetry Handbook,* by Mary Oliver

Living On the Edge

I sit.
Your big wide arms
welcome me
your style is
classic and strong.

A snowy egret glides
down the canal,
as a balmy breeze
floats over me.

My soul is calm,
the clouds
draw me into a trance.
My breathing slows,
eyes fixed.

I've found paradise
in my favorite
Adirondack chair,

here in the Keys,
living on the edge.

Deborah Linker

Orchids at Midnight

After the rain,
orchids at midnight
reach out to me
in warm, wet darkness.

Crickets chirp, fish jump
as soothing night
washes over me.

Memories lying here
under dancing stars,
ignite a wild passion,

your warm kisses
on the small of my neck,
two young and careless lovers
lost in touch,

a white orchid
on my bare skin
as you kissed away
sprinkles of rain.

Locked in the pain of losing you
I am forever
tethered
to these delicate orchids at midnight.

Listen

A whisper,
a flash of indecision,
fleeting thoughts
on wings of a hawk.

Whispers,
soft and low
whirled around my head
as I was sinking,
struggling to breathe.

Lessons were there
just above the surface.
I didn't listen.
I didn't still my mind.

Take in the light breeze
flowing over your body
in the quiet moonlit night
along water's edge.

A whisper
as gentle as the ripple of a wave
can be as powerful
as ocean's surf
crashing on the beach.

Fear

Fear, fear,
clutching fear
grabs at me

twisted emotions,
churning,
boiling

can't swallow
can't eat
sleep arrives
with wild dreams.

Should I go?
Should I stay?

Fear of being alone
fear of choosing
the wrong one

fear of money —
not enough
too much?

Fear of failure
fear of success

fear of old age
losing words.

The plane is
Sliding

d
o
w
n
w
a
r
d
s

and I'm the pilot.

Deborah Linker

Coming Home

Clutter, traffic,
people rushing
with no purpose,
photographs of a life
washed away,

a colorless
body of water
flowing under the
veneer.

I belong
to the open sea,
the tropical blue
a renewed path
on my island of dreams,

life is
slow,
calm,
moving as quietly
as a brown pelican
skimming
the surface.

Home is being
barefoot in the sand
watching sunsets
thoughts set adrift
forever moving.

The straight road ahead
tugs at my heart
pulling me forward
as the full moon rises
over the eastern atoll.

I am
coming home.

Strong as Lily

> for Lily Lawrence Bow, of Bow Channel,
> a Keys pioneer of the early 1900s.

Be strong they said, when I was only three,
wiping my cheeks as mama drove away.
You're strong, she needs me
said my young blond lover
when he left me at thirty-three.

Broken trust,
tears and lies
as pieces of my heart disappear
along life's cutting trail.

Be strong as Lily Bow
in the billowing winds of Cudjoe
growing limes to survive
and living off the sea.

Strong-willed she was
when her booze-loving man
hit the Northern road,
leaving two sons and a wife
among the mucky mangrove.

Years later
with thickened heart
and lost key,
I reach out with love,
but make sure nothing touches me.

Living on the Edge

Like Lily Bow,
at nature's heart
in the smudge fires of Cudjoe,
I am strong,
I am brave and
I am
alone.

Deborah Linker

Bonsai

The powerful bonsai
with wired branches
left in my care
was watered
protected from the cold.

In fear
I could not let my shears
touch its tender leaves

it grew wildly
out of control.

My friend,
a *crazymaker*,
moved on
said destiny
left the plant to me.

Slowly, a freedom
to trim, nurture
crept back to my hands
as my skill emerged

an ancient art
tamed and found
a beauty
that was always there.

Slack Tide

The murky water of
my canal stares at me,
no ebb, no flow.

A light summer rain
wets my face
while palm fronds
bend to the breeze.

Since we parted
my life has no
movement.

Seagrass pools in
the corners of my mind
as an anxious peace
awaits me, and
my soul enters
a slack tide.

Sounds Without Borders

Laughter of children playing
lovers kiss, whisper,
I wonder what they're saying,

giggles of young girls
barefoot on the grass
crying of a young boy
searching for his mom's hand

a group of women — buzzing bees
sharing tasty treats, crunchy bread,
bright red cherries and petite Madelines.

I sit in silence in this park so far from home
never uttering a sound,
see lovers, children, picnics and smiles,

lovely sounds
that have no borders,
I watch and understand.

Romance

Romantic love blindsides you
    like a lightning strike

Only to leave you
    at an unexpected moment,

Making you question
    what you saw in this person,

And your stomach turns
    with your heart racing

Not for the first kiss,
    but for your escape.

Could this be all there is?
    Happily

Ever after
    fades with rainbows.

Deborah Linker

Mighty Osprey

Standing guard
high on her throne
with black mask
white cap,

while her mate hovers
in warm currents
peers deep into the waters,
plunges with bullet speed
talons deep into its prey.

My silent kayak glides
too close for this mother's comfort
as high pitched squawks
paralyze my movements,

eyes peeled
to the woven nest in the sky,
in amazement, I watch
this mighty raptor of the sea

as she performs
her diversion flight to protect
her young — so strong, so devoted,
an unrelenting hunter for her babes.

And I wonder
about my mother,
and lessons she might have learned
from this mighty mangrove queen.

Living on the Edge

Gonna Fly

Standing on the
    edge
        nature flows

life passing me by
    leaving darkness
        seeing light

the weight has lifted
        my heart is
            free

I thought you got
        the best of me

now the rest of me
        is gonna fly.

"You can't wait for anything. Close your eyes, hold your breath, stay in one spot, you're still moving. Life is moving under you. There's no waiting."

—Movie, *Get Low* presented by K5 International

The Boss

Behind your cold glass desk
you sit in a plush leather chair,
tanned hide of some innocent animal,
on the phone, feet up,
laughing, flirting.

You look at me, eyes dark,
an empty stare
daring me to protest.

That toxic ring I've grown to hate
always puts me on hold
in the middle of a sentence,
a raised finger signals stop,

there it is – that smile, that charm
the twinkle in your eye,
not for me, it travels through the line
to some unknown entity.

There is no connection in this room.
Why does that little plastic phone
that clangors in our sinking existence
always demand the center of attention?

Sunset Dreams

I welcome the night
as I crawl between the soft sheets
and fall into a restless sleep
electrified with anticipation.
You emerge – pulsating, young, dark, hard.
I lay simmering, writhing as you enter
my dreams.

I fall back – young, soft, beautiful
again.
I dissolve into you.
We are silent like the night,
solid like the earth with passions stirring,
flying high together.

Don't go,
not yet my late night lover.
Dawn comes too soon,
I close my eyes
command you to stay.
The sun creeps across my face
as I reluctantly awake
breathlessly, heated in a pool of lust,
once again,
to face the sunset of my life.

Deborah Linker

Nickerbean

Your scrambling vine
with prickly pods and sharp spines
hidden under your leaves,
planted under a daughter's window
to ward off young lovers —

a father's wish
or an ancient
birth control?

Yellow butterflies eat your sweetness
while Scottish children wear
a necklace of your seeds
to keep evil away,

and medicine men steam tea
from your bark to fight malaria.

Worry stones, or good luck charms?
Tales or truth?
We may never know
of this persistent creeping vine

also called the holdback bush,
living up to its name
against disease, evil,
and a bit of the wild.

China

He longs for China
on high mountain tops
where old poets live.

Does he not know
his blood runs deep
with the open sea,
where blue meets blue?

Mountains are cold
as his heart would be
far from sounds of surf

and I as a lonely loon
would yearn
for his poetic words
to warm my day.

Don't go into the pale mist
my friend.
Your destiny is here,

where laughter and loss
pulse through your veins
and the bonefish
know your name.

Vanishing

This circle of passion,
a mark of commitment
fades before my eyes.

A pale emptiness remains
on my sun kissed skin,
as I face a half made bed
and a dinner for one.

I wonder,
when will this image,
twenty years in the making
disappear from my hand?

"They will think what they will, and let us leave them to their faulty logic, for what do we care finally when all is said and done."
— *Vindication,* by Frances Sherwood

Quiet Love

Waiting lifetimes
as a young maiden
    I searched for your familiar eyes.

When our souls met
on ancient shores
    seagrass was the bed.

In moonlight
you sailed away,
    a warrior of the sea.

Now, our thoughts mingle as one
surging with the ocean's
    rise and fall.

We talk, laugh, share,
your touch a movement away
    as hidden passions stir.

I crave to taste the sweetness of your words
the honeydew nectar which has escaped me for
    Ohhhhh so long.

Perhaps one day our waters will flow as one
cresting on the
    seventh wave.

For now,
I hide my love in
    this secret friendship,

daring not to seek what I desire
for you belong to her
    and I to another.

As You Sleep

I lay here quietly
waiting for your
slow cadence of gentle breathing.

I let go – my clenched fists relax
my space, my magical night awaits me
as I throw open the doors and welcome the sea.

I taste salt air
forget my doom-filled days
run barefoot on the wet shore

as chains that held me fall away
and surf's fairy dust scatters about
while you lay sleeping all the while.

Twilight is on the horizon,
hopeful, my day soon turns into night.
I hasten before you awake, clinging

to my side of the bed to drift into dreams
of a bird taking flight, stepping off,
floating gently out of sight.

Still Stalking

In golden slippers
he slow dances
across quiet waters
of red mangroves

as the setting sun
casts a purple haze
on his powder-white reflection.

A snowy egret
still stalking
with infinite patience,
and sliding strides.

Will startled prey satisfy
his hunger tonight?
Or will he retreat
to heavy thickets

once again
with familiar emptiness
in his belly?

Deborah Linker

Last Time I Cried

My father died
the first day of autumn,
a warm Kentucky morn.

An undammed river flowed
as I held his lifeless hand,
kissed his cheek.
How he hated the cold.

No more fishing trips,
camping under stars, or
water skiing on mirrored lakes,
his smile a burned memory in my mind.

Unrealized childhood moments
I was sure I was the smarter one.
Now, age reveals how his wisdom
touches my life today.

In a graveyard behind a church
built by his own hands
under spreading oak branches
yellow roses are laid
looking out on a lake where we played.

I am my father's daughter,
his strength, endurance and
love of water passed to me.
How I long to share one more day
on this tropical paradise I call home.

Living on the Edge

Pain, sorrow and anger
have pulsed through my life
since the day he slipped away,
hidden secrets from my father's eyes —

but the last time I cried
was when my daddy died.

Deborah Linker

Salty Queen

> For the historical old Seven Mile bridge that spans from
> Knights Key to Pigeon Key

A mighty spirit rises
from her beautiful
concrete pillars
and arches

with an infinite pathway
enticing us,
suspended
over a world of blue
past and present blended
swirling waters flowing beneath.

Listen,

in quietness,
among
gliding pelicans
and sunning cormorants,

you will hear the whistle
of Flagler's East Coast train
slowing down
at Knight's Key
to make the curve
on the Old Seven

with children laughing,
people pointing in awe
at the wonders of the sea,
as they traverse a different time.

What will be her demise,
this old salty queen
with cracked skin,
rusty bones and
coconut pavement?

Will she fade away
in the crimson sunset
or one mystic sunrise,
fragment by fragment
carried out to the deep?

I think not.

For the Old Seven
is of the Conch Republic,

and this majestic treasure
has an everlasting beat
in the heart
of the Florida Keys.

Nourishment

Mourning doves,
chubby balls of feather
huddle near my door
waiting,

motionless,
across the garden,
their bowl
overflows with seed.
Why don't they move?

Like the doves,
I am moments away
from nourishment,
not moving.

A wall
around the hole in my chest
where my heart is locked
keeps me frozen in place.

I long for eagle's vision
frigate's shrewdness
and the gentleness of a dove
as I will one day feed again

on life's lessons
forever searching
heightened, with every
movement
soaring to new worlds.

Seasoned Passion

A resting volcano,
not a hatchling
nor a babe,
a tamed lioness
with seasoned passion

waiting for you
to connect
to roll in the deep,
ride on the waves

a teacher, not a student
a taster of fruit
ripe and plump.

Come to me with haste
my love,
before the
winter sun covers me
with an unwelcomed stillness
and dancing stars disappear
behind a tainted veil.

Nicholas Matcovich

Son of Russia,
father of seven,
a hermit,
arrived in No Name,

sent his wife to Key West
to roll cigars,
while he tended crops
by water's edge.

Some call him crazy
others say it was talent
as they all envied
his bountiful harvest.

Precious sapodillas,
guarded with guns,
even Dr. Fairchild tasted
fruits envied by all.

Fierce winds, heat and rumors
did not oppress this mysterious loner
lived to ninety-two, loved
buried gold rather than glitter.

Mad hermit
of No Name,
I tip my hat to you,
think you had it right.

Why do we brand a person
That trusts plants more than man,
what we touch, taste not hear?

Whenever I am asked
who is one now gone, that
I wish I could have met.

I would answer
with secret admiration,
Nicolas Matcovich,
hermit farmer of No Name Key.

Deborah Linker

Mentor

He wades at water's edge
as his father and father's father
in different waters, but same.

He cast his line
in shadows of black mangroves
the goal – the elusive one.

Teach me I said,
I want to learn,
transfer this skill to me.

He slowly turned with a wise look
upon his face,
shook his head gently, and said,

if the wind is right,
and water clear,
and you're lucky enough to see one

cast your line
in just the right spot
next to one you desire.

Pray he'll see
your lure swimming by
hungry enough to take it,

and lucky enough
to land this one
before a shark can snag him.

Living on the Edge

But the joy my dear,
he softly whispered,
is to hold this beauty so near

then watch him sprint
back to hidden shadows,
released to swim again.

I'm lucky enough
to have known you my friend,
as he guided my hand on the water.

Before Dawn

Right before dawn,
when light
is trapped
between night and day,
I chase my dreams back to
unknown places of paradise.

My heart throbs loudly
against the silence,
as I awake from fitful sleep.
Nature's fire floods the room,
and once again,
I long for you.

For Charlie

> February 25, 1945 – August 20, 2011

It's not what she wanted,
not what she planned
with an unexpected knock on the door.

Stopped in her tracks
with dreams and plans halted
when life dealt this rotten hand.

There's nowhere to hide
no escape from the pain
when someone you love,
your soulmate is dying.

Her sweet tearful songs
as friends said goodbye
he slowly slipped away.

"I want to go with you,"
I heard her say,
and part of her died that day.

He sailed away as a turbulent storm
rattled against the dark
bolts of light filled the room
his scent lingered above

and thunder echoed
"I'm okay."

Carrousel of Life

I don't know what to say.
I don't know what to do.
I'm always the strong one,
and now I feel helpless.

I dare to have these thoughts,
my worries, in the face of your tragedy?
I'm a writer
lost for words to comfort you.

What do I say to my friend
sitting by her husband's side,
her soulmate,
as a dreadful disease hovers?

Do I stay upbeat,
bring you laughter with
my stupid jokes,
bake you an apple pie?

Do I help you navigate
through this fog
as we dare to speak
of the unknown future.

I want to tell you
I care, be strong, I'll be there for you,
but I fear these overused clichés
cannot pierce your
wall of sorrow and pain.

Living on the Edge

When this carrousel of life
ends my friend,
and the circus music fades,
we will cry, laugh,
and love once again.

Shattered

As I hit the wall
glass shattered
tossed jagged pieces
of life about.

In your hand
my heart stopped beating
when a door slammed
in my house of dreams.

My once in a lifetime
has faded.
I'm out on the road
once again

as I cut a channel,
through this ocean,
to dodge pirates and
thieves of love.

Last Hug

Our arms intertwined,
a lifetime of memories
flashed before my eyes.

I tasted salt on your neck
felt your heart pulse,
and slowly stepped back.

You released your grip,
rings clinked
as they fell from my hand.

I drove away
not looking back,
my uncertain future lay ahead.

A lone albatross
drifting in sands of time,
I am forever changed.

Cold Bed

Soft caresses,
heated kisses
skin on skin,
an invitation
for afternoon delight
have never crossed this bed,

this cold bed
a refuge from lies,
deceit.

Like a soldier
who leaves a battlefield
I withdraw from love.

My passion flower
traded for a bed of peace,

for is it not better
to be alone,
than lonely
with someone you love?

Deadly Manchineel

Shiny green leaves
with no thorns as warnings
its small death apple,
tasty they say

but sweetness turns to fire
when this poison fruit
slips through your lips
charring your throat

dripping rain
through branches
triggers burns
and blisters.

Indians knew
crushing leaves
in their enemies'
drinking water,

listening on shore for
shrieks to quiescent,
Spanish invaders
tied to its branches.

This tropical tree does not
easily reveal, its secret known to few,
he who sleeps with the **Manchineel**
indeed will sleep forever.

Late Night Lover

A world of blue flows
in front of her,
        as she lays
on the sand,
        by her side
a chilled bottle
        of wine.

Her heart grows
        anxious
as the sun sets,
innocence
        abandoned
she knows
  this is the night
      he'll appear.

A blanket
      of night mist
covers her body,
dense clouds
  mask a sliver
        of a moon
hiding
   a sailor's
       night light.

She shivers,
      reaches out
to touch
     silence,

Living on the Edge

sips
    the last drop
        of wine.

So many forgotten
yesterdays
with broken
      tomorrows,

love and pain,
the same,
      all faded
with the cooing
of white
    crowned
        pigeons.

The strike of midnight,
    with hazed clarity

can she face
    the long walk home?

Turning Fifty-Nine

My mind whirled
    as the train passed by,
        my body swerved.

Should I get on?
    A trickle of fear
        traveled down my spine.

Then suddenly,
    an open door
    as car fifty-nine approached.

Oh what the hell,
    I jumped on board.

Watch out world,
    the best year of my life
        is coming down the tracks.

"He turned and looked at her, and she grew uncomfortable again under his gaze, though she didn't feel as if he were looking at her as a woman, the way a woman might want if it was the right man. She felt she'd gone past the age for that and into a settled middle age. It was a passing she'd mourned, then gotten over."

—"Into Silence" by Marlin Barton

Living on the Edge

Chillin' in the Keys

Chillin' in the tropics
in the warm palm breeze

sippin' on a cool drink
with flying sails not sleighs.

Worries seem to disappear
as footprints in the sand

and Santa slowly sways
with the steel drum band.

Soon the tourist, young and old
embrace the sun,
forget the snow.

Reindeer replaced by
dolphins and manatees.

Christmas in the Keys
is the place for me.

previously published in the, Marathon Weekly, December 24, 2011, "Holiday Poem Winners."

About the Author

Deborah Linker, born in Owensboro, Kentucky in 1952, received her master's degree in speech-language pathology from Murray State University. The website, Rocky Road Adventures, available at www.deborahclinker.com, was created by Deborah, where she blogs about her adventures and discoveries along life's journey. She is actively involved in the Big Pine Writer's Group and the Key West Poetry Guild.

She is the moderator of the "Open Mic Poetry Jam" she initiated at the Marathon Public Library, and co-author of the program, "Poetry of the Keys."

An avid scuba diver, trained volunteer at the Dolphin Research Center, member of Paradise Peddlers and Paddlers, she recently joined efforts to save the historic Old Seven Mile Bridge with the Friends of Old Seven organization.

Deborah resides in Marathon, which she considers one of the jewels of the Florida Keys.

Resources

Here is a list for additional information about the history and nature of the Florida Keys:

Florida State Parks. http://www.floridaStateParks.org/

Friends of Old Seven, Inc. http://www.friendsofoldseven.org/

Hammer, Roger. *Florida Keys Wildflowers*, Guilford, Connecticut and Helena, Montanta, The Global Pequot Press, 2004.

Historic photos. http://bit.ly/kwhistory

Parks, Pat. *The Railroad that Died at Sea*, Marathon, Florida, The Ketch & Yawl Press, 1968.

Standiford, Les. *Last Train to Paradise*, New York, New York: Three Rivers Press, 2002.

Tom's Keys History Blog. http://www.keyslibraries.org/

Viele, John. The *Florida Keys A History of the Pioneeers*, Sarasota, Florida: Pineapple Press, 1996.

Wilkinson, Jerry. http://www.keyshistory.org/